Fingerlings™

MAD LIBS JUNIOR

by Mickie Matheis

Mad Libs
An Imprint of Penguin Random House

MAD LIBS
Penguin Young Readers Group
An Imprint of Penguin Random House LLC

Mad Libs format copyright © 2018 by Penguin Random House LLC. All rights reserved.

Concept created by Roger Price & Leonard Stern

WowWee.

Fingerlings® and all product names, designations and logos are trademarks of WowWee Group Limited.
Copyright © 2016–2018 WowWee Group Limited. All rights reserved.

Published by Mad Libs,
an imprint of Penguin Random House LLC,
345 Hudson Street, New York, New York 10014.
Printed in the USA.

ISBN 9781524791742
1 3 5 7 9 10 8 6 4 2

MAD LIBS ☺ JUNIOR.
INSTRUCTIONS

MAD LIBS JUNIOR® is a game for kids who don't like games!
It can be played by one, two, three, four, or forty.

RIDICULOUSLY SIMPLE DIRECTIONS:

At the top of each page in this book, you will find four columns of words, each headed by a symbol. Each symbol represents a part of speech. The symbols are:

★	☺	➡	?
NOUNS	**ADJECTIVES**	**VERBS**	**MISC.**

MAD LIBS JUNIOR® is fun to play with friends, but you can also play it by yourself! To begin, look at the story on the page below. When you come to a blank space in the story, look at the symbol that appears underneath. Then find the same symbol on this page and pick a word that appears below the symbol. Put that word in the blank space, and cross out the word, so you don't use it again. Continue doing this throughout the story until you've filled in all the spaces. Finally, read your story aloud and laugh!

EXAMPLE:

"Goodbye!" he said, as he jumped into his ＿＿＿＿＿＿＿ and ＿＿＿＿＿＿＿
★ ➡

off with his pet ＿＿＿＿＿＿＿.
?

★	☺	➡	?
NOUNS	**ADJECTIVES**	**VERBS**	**MISC.**
car	curly	drove	hamster
boat	purple	~~danced~~	dog
roller skate	wet	drank	cat
taxicab	tired	twirled	~~giraffe~~
~~surfboard~~	silly	swam	monkey

"Goodbye!" he said, as he jumped into his **SURFBOARD** and **DANCED**
★ ➡

off with his pet **GIRAFFE**.
?

MAD LIBS ☺ JUNIOR.
QUICK REVIEW

In case you haven't learned about the parts of speech yet, here is a quick lesson:

A **NOUN** ★ is the name of a person, place, or thing. *Sidewalk, umbrella, bathtub,* and *roller skates* are nouns.

An **ADJECTIVE** ☺ describes a person, place, or thing. *Lumpy, soft, ugly, messy,* and *short* are adjectives.

A **VERB** ➜ is an action word. *Run, jump,* and *swim* are verbs.

MISC. **?** can be any word at all. Some examples of a word that could be miscellaneous are: *nose, monkey, five,* and *blue.*

MAD LIBS JUNIOR® is fun to play with friends, but you can also play it by yourself! To begin, look at the story on the page below. When you come to a blank space in the story, look at the symbol that appears underneath. Then find the same symbol on this page and pick a word that appears below the symbol. Put that word in the blank space, and cross out the word, so you don't use it again. Continue doing this throughout the story until you've filled in all the spaces. Finally, read your story aloud and laugh!

THUMBS-UP FOR THE FINGERLINGS

★ NOUNS	☺ ADJECTIVES	➡ VERBS	? MISC.
bucket	chunky	snore	chipmunks
spaceship	valuable	text	walruses
ant	hairy	drive	chickadees
rainbow	lazy	shovel	lizards
pillow	invisible	chomp	elephants
seesaw	loud	skate	bunnies
flower	pointy	chat	pigeons
banana	shiny	twinkle	turtles
flag	wooden	swing	roosters
penny	starry	cook	lobsters
couch	hilarious	shop	pigs
notebook	polka-dotted	explode	donkeys

MAD LIBS JUNIOR.

THUMBS-UP FOR THE FINGERLINGS

Have you heard of the Fingerlings? They are super-cute little

_____ **?** who want to be your _____ ☺ friends!

The leader of the _____ ☺ group is Bella the monkey.

She's an energetic _____ ★ who will bounce and flip and

_____ ➡ like a gymnast. Bella has a twin named Boris who

dreams about becoming a/an _____ ☺ rock star. This silly

_____ ★ likes to pretend he's drumming on a/an _____ ★

for thousands of screaming _____ **?** . Then there's

Marge, a totally laid-back, _____ ☺ sloth who will always

_____ ➡ . . . very . . . very . . . slowly. And Gigi the unicorn

is the most glamorous of all the _____ **?** . She loves to pose

and _____ ➡ in front of any camera! When the Fingerlings

are around, fun and friendship are right at your fingertips!

MAD LIBS JUNIOR® is fun to play with friends, but you can also play it by yourself! To begin, look at the story on the page below. When you come to a blank space in the story, look at the symbol that appears underneath. Then find the same symbol on this page and pick a word that appears below the symbol. Put that word in the blank space, and cross out the word, so you don't use it again. Continue doing this throughout the story until you've filled in all the spaces. Finally, read your story aloud and laugh!

WELCOME TO MELODY VILLAGE

★ NOUNS	☺ ADJECTIVES	➡ VERBS	? MISC.
guitars	furry	launch	library
blankets	dopey	scrub	airport
treetops	stinky	whistle	grocery store
spoons	flat	stretch	museum
computers	bouncy	frown	school
kites	green	scamper	closet
hammers	curious	swim	castle
pockets	chilly	twist	doghouse
gnomes	brave	collapse	gas station
snowballs	pretty	shout	bathroom
skateboards	slippery	cough	graveyard
hairbrushes	greasy	blink	fun house

MAD LIBS JUNIOR.
WELCOME TO MELODY VILLAGE

Do you want to visit a charming little _____ where you

can see _____ sights and _____ with friendly

residents? Then come explore Melody Village, home of the

_____ Fingerlings. If you love to _____ in the

great outdoors, check out our beautifully _____

_____ with a playground, a swimming pool, and gardens

full of flowering _____ . Watch a play or hear a band

_____ at our grand old concert hall. Try some local treats

at the Banana Shack. It's where all the cool _____ like to

_____ . The owner, Ollie the monkey, makes all kinds of

delicious, drinkable _____ from bananas. No matter where

you wander around Melody Village, you'll get a _____

welcome from the _____ who _____ there.

MAD LIBS JUNIOR® is fun to play with friends, but you can also play it by yourself! To begin, look at the story on the page below. When you come to a blank space in the story, look at the symbol that appears underneath. Then find the same symbol on this page and pick a word that appears below the symbol. Put that word in the blank space, and cross out the word, so you don't use it again. Continue doing this throughout the story until you've filled in all the spaces. Finally, read your story aloud and laugh!

A BUSY DAY FOR BELLA

★ NOUNS	☺ ADJECTIVES	➡ VERBS	? MISC.
dust	fuzzy	snorkeling	yee-haw
shoelaces	confusing	breathing	gadzooks
hair dryers	dark	dialing	shazam
trophies	crunchy	golfing	eureka
teddy bears	enormous	sneezing	darn tootin'
screwdrivers	frightening	farming	woo-hoo
race cars	flaky	floating	ahoy there
candy bars	annoying	grilling	yippee
pom-poms	clumsy	nodding	yuck
paper clips	fantastic	knitting	sweet
balloons	exhausted	jiggling	brilliant
statues	frilly	disappearing	fabulous

MAD LIBS JUNIOR.
A BUSY DAY FOR BELLA

Bella is a busy, _____ Fingerling! She bounces out

of bed and greets each day with a happy "_____."

Then she has breakfast, the most _____ meal of the

day. Bella likes to eat fresh _____ and a smoothie

mixed with crushed _____—_____, that's

delicious! Exercise is also very important to Bella, and she gets

that by _____ on her trampoline. Then she does chores

like _____ at the store and cleaning her _____

room. Bella always makes sure to spend time _____ with

her family and her _____. She keeps a to-do list on

her _____ phone, and every time she completes a task,

her phone goes "_____"! Nothing beats a day of

getting stuff done. For Bella, a busy day is the best kind of day!

MAD LIBS JUNIOR® is fun to play with friends, but you can also play it by yourself! To begin, look at the story on the page below. When you come to a blank space in the story, look at the symbol that appears underneath. Then find the same symbol on this page and pick a word that appears below the symbol. Put that word in the blank space, and cross out the word, so you don't use it again. Continue doing this throughout the story until you've filled in all the spaces. Finally, read your story aloud and laugh!

ROCK STAR LIFE

★ NOUNS	☺ ADJECTIVES	→ VERBS	? MISC.
basketballs	goofy	dancing	burritos
tissues	terrible	baking	pineapples
hats	teeny	somersaulting	cookies
telephones	lumpy	snorting	watermelons
canaries	ticklish	drinking	sandwiches
clocks	wavy	shampooing	waffles
wagons	burnt	digging	pizzas
sneakers	noisy	polishing	milkshakes
mattresses	cranky	rolling	tomatoes
nickels	bedazzled	shaking	hamburgers
napkins	magical	diving	mushrooms
toothbrushes	sleepy	flying	pickles

MAD LIBS JUNIOR.
ROCK STAR LIFE

Ever since he was a young monkey, Boris has dreamed of

becoming a _____ drummer. He even has a name for

his future rock band—the _____ _____ ?. Boris

has it all planned for himself and his best _____! The

group will become _____ all over the world, appear

on TV, radio, and billboards, and have their own flavor of

_____ ?. Boris likes to imagine his face _____ →

inside neon _____ in concert halls. It makes him

happy to think about _____ → up onstage in front of

a _____ → audience full of all his best _____ .

Boris loves the idea of being famous—and not just for the

adoring _____ that would ask him to autograph their

_____ . He loves the idea of being paid in _____ ?!

MAD LIBS JUNIOR® is fun to play with friends, but you can also play it by yourself! To begin, look at the story on the page below. When you come to a blank space in the story, look at the symbol that appears underneath. Then find the same symbol on this page and pick a word that appears below the symbol. Put that word in the blank space, and cross out the word, so you don't use it again. Continue doing this throughout the story until you've filled in all the spaces. Finally, read your story aloud and laugh!

THE PERFECT SELFIE, BY GIGI

★ NOUNS	☺ ADJECTIVES	➡ VERBS	? MISC.
scissors	groovy	wrestle	big toe
motorcycles	ordinary	nibble	kidney
aprons	hungry	rake	elbow
fire hydrants	funny	joust	pinkie
helicopters	bossy	fish	nose
chairs	droopy	dust	forehead
skillets	ripped	paint	kneecap
planets	spicy	snooze	earlobe
worms	blue	roller skate	eyebrow
aliens	wobbly	cartwheel	belly button
pianos	puffy	waddle	tongue
bracelets	handsome	juggle	tooth

MAD LIBS ☺ JUNIOR.
THE PERFECT SELFIE, BY GIGI

Hiya, I'm Gigi, and I'm here to teach you all how to take

_____ selfies. So, go grab your cam, fam, and
   ☺

follow these _____ steps for getting great photos of
              ☺

your gorgeous _____ .
              ?

1. Wear your cutest _____ and make sure your
                    ★

_____ is styled and fabulous.
   ?

2. _____ for the camera! And smile, too! Show off
   →

your pretty white _____ .
                  ★

3. Add some filters so that your _____ is covered with
                                ?

bright red hearts or smiling _____ . You'll look as
                            ★

awesomely _____ as I always do!
          ☺

4. Post your pic! This will help you get a ton of _____
                                                ★

who want to _____ with you—and follow you, too!
           →

MAD LIBS JUNIOR® is fun to play with friends, but you can also play it by yourself! To begin, look at the story on the page below. When you come to a blank space in the story, look at the symbol that appears underneath. Then find the same symbol on this page and pick a word that appears below the symbol. Put that word in the blank space, and cross out the word, so you don't use it again. Continue doing this throughout the story until you've filled in all the spaces. Finally, read your story aloud and laugh!

SLOW-MOTION MARGE

★ NOUNS	☺ ADJECTIVES	➡ VERBS	? MISC.
ice cubes	stormy	drive	picnicking
airplanes	grumpy	yell	napping
tables	filthy	bump	squeezing
spatulas	boring	sew	marching
coasters	soft	steer	scratching
pictures	rubbery	breathe	stirring
fences	flexible	waddle	doodling
robots	purple	unlock	scooting
scarecrows	scary	lean	knocking
fire trucks	speedy	crawl	twirling
surfboards	gigantic	write	nudging
clouds	kooky	sing	jumping

Marge the sloth moves super slowly. Her friends can't get her

to _____ ➡ any faster—ever! The others often find her

_____ ? quietly in the grass or _____ ? upside

down on a tree branch, trying to spot _____ shapes in

the clouds. Marge also loves to read all kinds of _____ ★.

In fact, she often volunteers to _____ ➡ during story time

at the library. Her favorite book is *Goodnight,* _____

Sloth. In the story, a sloth says goodnight to a pair of slippers,

a _____ teddy bear, a painting of _____ ★,

and everything else in her room. By the time the sleepy sloth

finishes, it's morning! The parents of the _____ ★ listening

at the library love Marge. When she finishes _____ ?,

their little ones are fast asleep and _____ ?, too!

MAD LIBS JUNIOR® is fun to play with friends, but you can also play it by yourself! To begin, look at the story on the page below. When you come to a blank space in the story, look at the symbol that appears underneath. Then find the same symbol on this page and pick a word that appears below the symbol. Put that word in the blank space, and cross out the word, so you don't use it again. Continue doing this throughout the story until you've filled in all the spaces. Finally, read your story aloud and laugh!

TARA HEATS IT UP

★ NOUNS	☺ ADJECTIVES	→ VERBS	? MISC.
sticker	sugary	flip	combs
plunger	mellow	simmer	boxes
marshmallow	boiling	point	candles
book	suspicious	sail	sleeping bags
teapot	itchy	color	batteries
chalkboard	tasty	shake	diamonds
fire truck	pink	crash	coupons
stocking	glossy	explain	logs
toaster	heavy	steal	swimming pools
diaper	dusty	explore	pebbles
hose	massive	study	ballerinas
broom	creepy	giggle	refrigerators

MAD LIBS ⦿⦿ JUNIOR.
TARA HEATS IT UP

Being _____ friends with a fire-breathing _____ ⭐

like Tara is fun! Here's why:

1. Hungry for a snack? Tara can toast up _____ ⦿⦿

   treats like s'mores and grilled _____ ?.

2. Looking for adventure? You can _____ ➡ on her back

   for a/an _____ ⦿⦿ sightseeing tour over Melody Village,

   Blaze Mountain, and other amazing _____ ?.

3. Playing catch and get your _____ ⭐ stuck up in a tree?

   Tara can fly right up and rescue it.

4. Feeling chilly? She can easily light a campfire so you can

   _____ ➡ in front of it and warm up your _____ ?.

5. Need something for show-and- _____ ➡ at school?

   A dragon is the perfect _____ ⭐ to bring!

MAD LIBS JUNIOR® is fun to play with friends, but you can also play it by yourself! To begin, look at the story on the page below. When you come to a blank space in the story, look at the symbol that appears underneath. Then find the same symbol on this page and pick a word that appears below the symbol. Put that word in the blank space, and cross out the word, so you don't use it again. Continue doing this throughout the story until you've filled in all the spaces. Finally, read your story aloud and laugh!

FUN AT THE CLUBHOUSE

★ NOUNS	☺ ADJECTIVES	➜ VERBS	? MISC.
fireplace	rotten	skiing	megaphones
princess	skinny	crying	rockets
nugget	flashy	shuffling	sidewalks
chicken	topsy-turvy	cruising	scooters
backpack	famous	scribbling	pelicans
sandal	orange	humming	peanuts
jump rope	royal	spinning	lightbulbs
hat	sneaky	relaxing	televisions
iceberg	weird	skipping	forks
pumpkin	silent	dropping	letters
hedgehog	icy	tasting	microwaves
sailboat	smooth	staring	popcorn balls

MAD LIBS JUNIOR
FUN AT THE CLUBHOUSE

If you're in the mood for a/an _____ good time,

stop by to see Bella, Boris, and the other Fingerlings at their

super- _____ Clubhouse. Located in the center of

Melody Village, the Clubhouse is built among the branches of

a giant _____ tree. Every Fingerling has their own

_____ decorated with their favorite colors and

_____. Rooms are connected with _____

slides, bouncy trampolines, and _____ ladders.

There are common areas for eating, watching TV, or just

_____. The gang spends a lot of time at the

Clubhouse and especially enjoys _____ and hosting

_____ parties for their very best _____.

After all, there's no place like home.

MAD LIBS JUNIOR® is fun to play with friends, but you can also play it by yourself! To begin, look at the story on the page below. When you come to a blank space in the story, look at the symbol that appears underneath. Then find the same symbol on this page and pick a word that appears below the symbol. Put that word in the blank space, and cross out the word, so you don't use it again. Continue doing this throughout the story until you've filled in all the spaces. Finally, read your story aloud and laugh!

SWEET TIMES AT THE BANANA SHACK

★ NOUNS	☺ ADJECTIVES	➡ VERBS	? MISC.
T-shirts	windy	yawn	freckle
porches	frizzy	tumble	spleen
baseballs	obnoxious	squish	ankle
rugs	lacy	yank	ear
staplers	glamorous	holler	collarbone
raccoons	itchy	dream	arm
crayons	powerful	clean	mustache
firecrackers	strange	wish	armpit
bowls	absurd	hustle	thigh
noodles	yellow	doze	eyelash
robots	silly	skydive	cheek
sailors	jolly	vacuum	brain

MAD LIBS JUNIOR.

SWEET TIMES AT THE BANANA SHACK

Melody Village just got a little sweeter! The next time you have

a taste for a/an _____ frozen treat, _____

down to the Banana Shack, a cool new gathering spot run by

Ollie the monkey. Some of the fan favorites on the menu are:

- **Banana shakes:** Creamy and _____, these will

   make you rub your _____ and say, "Yummy!"
   ?

- **Smoothies:** This popular and _____ drink mixes

   bananas and fruit-flavored _____ . Put the
   ★

   straw up to your _____ and drink down
   ?

   the deliciousness!

- **Banana cones:** Eat these icy _____ before they
   ★

   melt—and before the Fingerling Minis can _____

   by and snatch them out of your _____!
   ?

Published by Mad Libs, an imprint of Penguin Random House LLC.

MAD LIBS JUNIOR® is fun to play with friends, but you can also play it by yourself! To begin, look at the story on the page below. When you come to a blank space in the story, look at the symbol that appears underneath. Then find the same symbol on this page and pick a word that appears below the symbol. Put that word in the blank space, and cross out the word, so you don't use it again. Continue doing this throughout the story until you've filled in all the spaces. Finally, read your story aloud and laugh!

ADVENTURES AT BLAZE MOUNTAIN

★ NOUNS	☺ ADJECTIVES	→ VERBS	? MISC.
piñatas	fluffy	decorate	teasing
flowerpots	pasty	sew	dreaming
saxophones	ridiculous	startle	sniffling
furnaces	slimy	swim	organizing
ribbons	polite	gargle	typing
toboggans	evil	vibrate	searching
newspapers	red	yodel	inventing
necklaces	hilly	film	surfing
water bottles	freezing	applaud	drawing
notebooks	nice	sing	flossing
hangers	patient	chew	bending
snowmen	woolly	exercise	camping

Whenever Bella, Boris, and Gigi are in the mood for a/an

_____ adventure, they always head to Blaze Mountain

to visit and spend time _____ with Tara the dragon.

Blaze Mountain is within _____ distance of Melody

Village, so the Fingerlings can easily _____ their

way there. Nestled in the mountains are castles made from

stone, metal, and _____. And the weather is always

perfect—sunny and _____! Tara loves when her

_____ friends come to her home to _____.

She starts a big bonfire outside on the deck so they can roast

_____ and toast _____. Then they go to one

of the many obstacle courses to see who can _____

the fastest. A day spent with Tara is always big fun!

MAD LIBS JUNIOR® is fun to play with friends, but you can also play it by yourself! To begin, look at the story on the page below. When you come to a blank space in the story, look at the symbol that appears underneath. Then find the same symbol on this page and pick a word that appears below the symbol. Put that word in the blank space, and cross out the word, so you don't use it again. Continue doing this throughout the story until you've filled in all the spaces. Finally, read your story aloud and laugh!

SIGN-UPS AT HARMONY STADIUM

★ NOUNS	☺ ADJECTIVES	➡ VERBS	? MISC.
rubber band	scrumptious	spying	lung
cage	dizzy	counting	thumb
earring	flowing	parking	neck
trumpet	musical	winning	ponytail
star	fiery	bowling	knuckle
ghost	black	melting	heel
place mat	glittery	spitting	lip
flashlight	sweaty	climbing	shoulder
fishbowl	swampy	hunting	tooth
sunflower	fresh	giggling	spine
toilet	leafy	imagining	toenail
roller coaster	shabby	spouting	eye

MAD LIBS JUNIOR.

SIGN-UPS AT HARMONY STADIUM

All Fingerlings are invited to Harmony Stadium to sign up for

a sports program. Whether you're good at running, dancing, or

water- _____ ➡ , we've got a _____ ☺ game for you!

• **Danceyball:** If you have rhythm in your _____ ?

and like _____ ➡ to music while waving around a

long _____ ★ , this is your sport! Unicorns are especially

good at Danceyball, but any _____ ★ can try it.

• **The Waterslide 500:** Go head-to- _____ ? with

the sloths in this splash-tastic event.

• **Trampoline Steeplechase:** Think you have _____ ☺

parkour skills? Try _____ ➡ through an obstacle

course covered in slippery _____ ★ peels! Make it

to the finish line without falling on your _____ ?!

MAD LIBS JUNIOR® is fun to play with friends, but you can also play it by yourself! To begin, look at the story on the page below. When you come to a blank space in the story, look at the symbol that appears underneath. Then find the same symbol on this page and pick a word that appears below the symbol. Put that word in the blank space, and cross out the word, so you don't use it again. Continue doing this throughout the story until you've filled in all the spaces. Finally, read your story aloud and laugh!

A VISIT TO THE FINGERLING MUSEUM OF HISTORY

★ NOUNS	☺ ADJECTIVES	→ VERBS	? MISC.
friends	smoky	hugging	1 million
rainbows	sloppy	hiding	0
boxes	soaked	washing	63½
beavers	nasty	arguing	17
pretzels	courageous	sleeping	40,000
baskets	lucky	gliding	0.9
toenails	damp	snacking	88
hamsters	fishy	sledding	562,903
trampolines	gooey	chopping	416
sandwiches	frustrating	snarling	2
eyelashes	prickly	zip-lining	33¼
fire hydrants	thirsty	dining	1,001

MAD LIBS JUNIOR.

A VISIT TO THE FINGERLING MUSEUM OF HISTORY

Today my class went on a field trip to the Fingerling Museum

of History, which the local _____ nicknamed

⭐

"the FINGMU." The outside of the building is decorated

with _____ statues of monkeys, unicorns, and

❓

other _____ . We spent _____ hours

⭐   ❓

_____ in the FINGMU and reading about the

➡️

_____ history of the Fingerlings. For example, I

😊

learned that Fingerlings were first discovered _____

➡️

in Melody Village nearly _____ years ago. Another

❓

fun fact is that the very first Fingerlings weren't little monkeys.

They were actually _____-foot-tall _____ . This

❓   ⭐

field trip wasn't just awesome—it was downright _____ !

😊

MAD LIBS JUNIOR® is fun to play with friends, but you can also play it by yourself! To begin, look at the story on the page below. When you come to a blank space in the story, look at the symbol that appears underneath. Then find the same symbol on this page and pick a word that appears below the symbol. Put that word in the blank space, and cross out the word, so you don't use it again. Continue doing this throughout the story until you've filled in all the spaces. Finally, read your story aloud and laugh!

MONKEYING AROUND

★ NOUNS	☺ ADJECTIVES	➡ VERBS	? MISC.
mops	crazy	judge	porcupine
hammocks	speckled	stroll	alligator
lawn mowers	wicked	row	buffalo
zippers	cheerful	scream	firefly
ninjas	messy	race	lion
cameras	wrinkled	slip	turkey
waterfalls	sour	collapse	mole
hoodies	muddy	iron	platypus
wastebaskets	greedy	sketch	caterpillar
lunch boxes	quirky	garden	flamingo
earmuffs	cozy	shop	dolphin
paintings	fancy	hug	zebra

MAD LIBS JUNIOR.
MONKEYING AROUND

Bella and Boris argue, just like all brothers and _____ . ★

Bella: Boris, it's late and I'm trying to _____ now. →

I need to get up early in the morning to _____ . →

Can you please stop banging on those _____ ? ★

Boris: I'm practicing so someday I can _____ with my →

favorite band, the _____ _____ . It's my dream!

Bella: Do you know what my _____ dream is, Boris?

Boris: To tell every _____ in Melody Village that

you have a famously _____ brother?

Bella: No, Boris, to sleep. Do you know how I can do that?

Boris: Sure do, sis—just stop talking! And do that soon because

you're an awfully _____ little _____ ?

when you're tired.

MAD LIBS JUNIOR® is fun to play with friends, but you can also play it by yourself! To begin, look at the story on the page below. When you come to a blank space in the story, look at the symbol that appears underneath. Then find the same symbol on this page and pick a word that appears below the symbol. Put that word in the blank space, and cross out the word, so you don't use it again. Continue doing this throughout the story until you've filled in all the spaces. Finally, read your story aloud and laugh!

LET'S HEAR IT FOR THE HOOMANS

★ NOUNS	☺ ADJECTIVES	→ VERBS	? MISC.
jelly bean	proud	splashing	bathrobes
life vest	clueless	standing	underwear
pirate	zany	firefighting	swimsuits
unicycle	tired	boxing	pajamas
spoon	silver	moseying	socks
haunted house	flaky	winking	neckties
bluebird	playful	hunting	hiking boots
taco	cuddly	wiping	parkas
bandage	chocolaty	creeping	slippers
purse	fake	burping	tutus
feather	bubbly	printing	dresses
button	terrifying	cleaning	leggings

MAD LIBS JUNIOR.
LET'S HEAR IT FOR THE HOOMANS

Last night, the Fingerlings were on their feet as the popular

_____ band The Hoomans rocked the stage in Melody
⭐

Village. The _____ crowd was wearing Hoomans
😊

_____ and dancing and _____ in the aisles
?   ➡

all night. Everyone went wild when local _____
➡

sensation Boris the monkey made a guest appearance on the

drums. Dressed in glittery, gold _____
?

and wearing a _____ top hat, he played along to
😊

The Hoomans' hit song "Funky Monkey." At the end of the

song, every _____ in the Fingerling audience began
⭐

cheering and _____ . Bella jumped up onstage to
➡

give Boris a _____ bouquet of bananas. For once,
😊

she felt very proud to be his twin _____ .
⭐

MAD LIBS JUNIOR® is fun to play with friends, but you can also play it by yourself! To begin, look at the story on the page below. When you come to a blank space in the story, look at the symbol that appears underneath. Then find the same symbol on this page and pick a word that appears below the symbol. Put that word in the blank space, and cross out the word, so you don't use it again. Continue doing this throughout the story until you've filled in all the spaces. Finally, read your story aloud and laugh!

NOW PLAYING AT THE SIMI-PLEX

★ NOUNS	☺ ADJECTIVES	→ VERBS	? MISC.
squirt gun	extraordinary	howling	sunglasses
basket	rusty	tiptoeing	boogers
headband	scrawny	pedaling	spoons
ocean	shimmery	spelling	sausages
telescope	tight	snoring	submarines
tuba	cheap	off-roading	coconuts
dollhouse	unusual	farming	motorcycles
brick	foolish	nodding	mixing bowls
locker	bumpy	climbing	eggs
wind chime	graceful	snowboarding	windows
doorbell	tall	patting	snowblowers
fork	circular	clapping	handkerchiefs

MAD LIBS ◯◯ JUNIOR.
NOW PLAYING AT THE SIMI-PLEX

Grab a bucket of buttered _____ **?** , take a seat,

and check out these _____ ◯◯ movies:

• **Monkeys in Space**: Two brave _____ **?** blast off in a

banana-shaped rocket- _____ ★ and start _____ ➡

to save planet Earth from alien _____ **?** .

• **Glammerella**: A unicorn styles her _____ ◯◯ mane,

adds jeweled _____ **?** to her horn, and takes photos of

herself _____ ➡ with the handsome _____ ★ .

• **Snow White and the Seven Sloths**: A beautiful _____ ★

living with a band of _____ ◯◯ sloths falls under

a spell that can only be broken by a kiss from a princely

_____ ★ . (Note: This movie runs long because

the actors are slow.)

MAD LIBS JUNIOR® is fun to play with friends, but you can also play it by yourself! To begin, look at the story on the page below. When you come to a blank space in the story, look at the symbol that appears underneath. Then find the same symbol on this page and pick a word that appears below the symbol. Put that word in the blank space, and cross out the word, so you don't use it again. Continue doing this throughout the story until you've filled in all the spaces. Finally, read your story aloud and laugh!

TAKING IT SLOW AT SLOTH BEACH

★ NOUNS	☺ ADJECTIVES	➜ VERBS	? MISC.
hamper	lovely	paint	spines
pen	hardy	surprise	kneecaps
apple	disgusting	listen	armpits
beanbag	flavorful	freeze	foreheads
meatloaf	mushy	dress	muscles
bumblebee	awkward	glare	ears
lightning	curly	shiver	elbows
volleyball	average	skip	lungs
pitcher	gloomy	vacuum	fingernails
ice skate	perfect	bake	freckles
towel	fragrant	rehearse	eyebrows
cowboy hat	icy	sprinkle	teeth

When the temperature heats up and the Fingerlings want to

cool down, they'll head to Sloth Beach. There's crystal-clear

water to _____ ➡ in or to relax in on _____ ★ -shaped

floaties. There's beautiful white sand to _____ ➡ in. It

feels so _____ ☺ and squishy between your _____ ? !

There are super-slow waves that are so easy to catch and ride a

surf-_____ ★ on. The laid-back sloths and their friends

like to dip their _____ ? in the ocean and feel the

warmth of the _____ ★ 's rays on their _____ ? .

It's also fun to hunt for _____ ☺ shells or starfish that wash

ashore. There's so much to see and do in this _____ ☺

beach town. Once you visit Sloth Beach, you'll want to come

back and _____ ➡ all the time!

MAD LIBS JUNIOR® is fun to play with friends, but you can also play it by yourself! To begin, look at the story on the page below. When you come to a blank space in the story, look at the symbol that appears underneath. Then find the same symbol on this page and pick a word that appears below the symbol. Put that word in the blank space, and cross out the word, so you don't use it again. Continue doing this throughout the story until you've filled in all the spaces. Finally, read your story aloud and laugh!

BLOCK PARTY AT THE VINES

★ NOUNS	☺ ADJECTIVES	➡ VERBS	? MISC.
crayon	classy	read	meatballs
penguin	whiny	sleep	peas
rowboat	circular	cook	salad
boot	green	joke	french fries
emerald	expensive	fail	nachos
coffee cup	gassy	twirl	fish sticks
blender	sweet	tango	dumplings
tape measure	furious	scribble	hot dogs
wreath	gentle	crash	pizzas
snail	warm	fart	stew
faucet	silly	sneeze	pork chops
barrel	brown	whistle	fried chicken

MAD LIBS ☺ JUNIOR.
BLOCK PARTY AT THE VINES

Greetings, _____ friends!
              [☺]

It's been too _____ around here, so it's
              [☺]

time for a party with food and fun! We will provide grilled

_____ and banana cones. Gigi and her friends will
      ?

bring _____-shaped piñatas stuffed with candy
          ★

_____ and will set up an area where you can
      ?

_____ in front of the camera. The sloths have promised
     ➡

to bring leaf tacos topped with bug-flavored _____ and
                                              ?

are organizing a relay race where the last one to _____
                                                        ➡

at the finish line wins! There will be other games, too, like hide-

and-_____ and _____-ball. Hope you can
       ➡   ★

come! A/An _____ time will be had by all!
              [☺]

Your _____ neighbors, Bella and Boris
        [☺]

MAD LIBS JUNIOR® is fun to play with friends, but you can also play it by yourself! To begin, look at the story on the page below. When you come to a blank space in the story, look at the symbol that appears underneath. Then find the same symbol on this page and pick a word that appears below the symbol. Put that word in the blank space, and cross out the word, so you don't use it again. Continue doing this throughout the story until you've filled in all the spaces. Finally, read your story aloud and laugh!

FINGERLING MINIS

★ NOUNS	☺ ADJECTIVES	➡ VERBS	? MISC.
dimes	silly	swaying	4
elves	joyful	floating	912
rulers	sleepy	pointing	100.5
frames	energetic	describing	1 million
soccer balls	chubby	complaining	0.2
spatulas	friendly	shimmying	3,758
radios	fancy	break dancing	0
signs	nerdy	giggling	50
harmonicas	important	camping	456,789
goggles	gross	flirting	18
doors	chewy	snoozing	250½
tulips	purple	kicking	10

Who are the Fingerling Minis? These mischievous _____ ★

travel in groups of up to _____ ? and don't know when

to stop _____ ➡ . Here are some examples of the chaos

they've already caused today—and it's only _____ ? o'clock!

• Stole Gigi's cell phone and took a group selfie while

_____ ➡ and shaking their _____ ☺ butts

• Stole _____ ? banana cones from _____ ★ in the

Banana Shack—and _____ ? of those cones belonged

to poor Boris

• Then stole drumsticks out of Boris's _____ ★ —right

before his _____ ☺ drum solo

The Minis are the biggest little troublemaking _____ ★

in Melody Village!

MAD LIBS JUNIOR® is fun to play with friends, but you can also play it by yourself! To begin, look at the story on the page below. When you come to a blank space in the story, look at the symbol that appears underneath. Then find the same symbol on this page and pick a word that appears below the symbol. Put that word in the blank space, and cross out the word, so you don't use it again. Continue doing this throughout the story until you've filled in all the spaces. Finally, read your story aloud and laugh!

BELLA BREAKS A RECORD

★ NOUNS	☺ ADJECTIVES	➡ VERBS	? MISC.
fan	scared	vaulting	noses
banjo	spotless	swishing	mouths
mirror	sticky	prancing	ears
nail	gray	braiding	arms
bicycle	positive	sniffling	ankles
bed	chatty	dripping	necks
skunk	heavy	clipping	backs
umbrella	spiky	sailing	shoulders
freezer	rude	riding	hands
merry-go-round	neat	counting	stomachs
staircase	dreary	sliding	elbows
ceiling fan	poor	blow-drying	knees

MAD LIBS JUNIOR.
BELLA BREAKS A RECORD

Hey, fam! This is Gigi, live and _____ from the Banana

Shack. Today, our very own jumpy _____, Bella,

was in the middle of trying to break the world record for

the most _____ in a single day when she heard

some _____ news. Ilsa Jumpanov, the famous

_____ gymnast, was in town! Bella immediately put

on a/an _____ with Ilsa's smiling face on the front,

strapped a pair of _____ shoes to her _____,

and bounced outside to find her _____ hero. Soon, Ilsa

came _____ along—and guess what? She had bouncing

_____ shoes strapped on, too! The monkeys leaned

their _____ in close and took a photo together. That

awesome moment made Bella "hashtag _____!"

MAD LIBS JUNIOR® is fun to play with friends, but you can also play it by yourself! To begin, look at the story on the page below. When you come to a blank space in the story, look at the symbol that appears underneath. Then find the same symbol on this page and pick a word that appears below the symbol. Put that word in the blank space, and cross out the word, so you don't use it again. Continue doing this throughout the story until you've filled in all the spaces. Finally, read your story aloud and laugh!

THE (CANDY) LAND OF THE UNICORNS

★ NOUNS	☺ ADJECTIVES	➡ VERBS	? MISC.
trees	cloudy	cartwheel	granola bars
cucumbers	buttery	swing	melons
stamps	upside-down	hopscotch	omelets
puppets	curvy	mix	bologna slices
water bottles	short	sketch	ice cream
arrows	artistic	tap dance	hamburgers
dishwashers	tiny	roll	pies
gold coins	funky	frolic	pizzas
quilts	moldy	snowboard	spaghetti
knights	microscopic	fetch	potato salad
tents	starry	dodge	tuna fish
ladybugs	fried	skip	spinach

MAD LIBS JUNIOR.
THE (CANDY) LAND OF THE UNICORNS

The Fingerlings are always excited to visit the unicorns who

_____→ in Sparkle Heights. No matter what time of year it

is, the weather there is deliciously _____☺. For example, the

powerful Santa Banana winds make the air smell like yummy

_____? mixed with chocolate chip _____★. During the

rainy season, it pours down gumdrops the size of _____★,

but this helps the orchards of _____☺ lollipops and the

fields of licorice-flavored _____? grow. When it's sunny,

there are plenty of fluffy popcorn _____★ to pick up and

munch. It's fun to _____→ outside when the sky is filled

with cotton candy _____★. There are even rainbow glaciers

where the unicorns make _____☺ snow cones. Going to

Sparkle Heights to _____→ for a day is truly a treat!

MAD LIBS JUNIOR® is fun to play with friends, but you can also play it by yourself! To begin, look at the story on the page below. When you come to a blank space in the story, look at the symbol that appears underneath. Then find the same symbol on this page and pick a word that appears below the symbol. Put that word in the blank space, and cross out the word, so you don't use it again. Continue doing this throughout the story until you've filled in all the spaces. Finally, read your story aloud and laugh!

WANTED: FINGERLING FRIENDS

★ NOUNS	☺ ADJECTIVES	→ VERBS	? MISC.
curtains	nervous	jump	barbecuing
folders	colorful	sneeze	somersaulting
checkers	bratty	wheeze	sawing
hippos	generous	twirl	inventing
balloons	unforgettable	backflip	collapsing
compasses	scaly	burp	skipping
paintbrushes	scratchy	stand	bicycling
lights	tall	salute	munching
packages	small	cheer	listening
rocking chairs	medium	explode	spying
slugs	slushy	pirouette	decorating
sponges	cheesy	gallop	jiggling

MAD LIBS JUNIOR.
WANTED: FINGERLING FRIENDS

Would you enjoy _____ with monkeys, sloths,

?

unicorns, and other _____ every day? Does a

★

clubhouse filled with _____ slides and rope ladders

☺

sound like your dream home? Could _____ in a

?

town where music, fun, and banana _____ are around

★

every corner make you feel happy and _____? If

☺

so, then YOU could be a Fingerling Friend! Melody Village is

looking for a few new _____ to play with, laugh with,

★

and _____ with. If you believe that friendship is

➡

right at your fingertips, then the _____ job of a

☺

Fingerling Friend might be right for you. _____

➡

today for an application!